KU-273-609

THE ILLUSTRATED POETS

Emily Dickinson

EDITED BY
Daniel Burnstone

PARRAGON

This is a Parragon Book.
Produced by Magpie Books,
an imprint of Robinson Publishing, London

Parragon
Unit 13-17, Avonbridge Trading Estate,
Atlantic Road, Avonmouth,
Bristol, BS11 9QD

Reprinted 1996

This book is sold subject to the condition that it shall not,
by way of trade or otherwise, be lent, resold, hired out or
otherwise circulated without the publisher's prior consent
in any form of binding or cover than that in which it is
published and without similar condition being imposed on
the subsequent purchaser.

Collection copyright © Parragon Book Service Ltd 1994

Cover picture: *Destiny*, 1900, by John William
Waterhouse, Towneley Hall Art Gallery & Museum,
Burnely/Bridgeman Art Library. Illustrations courtesy of:
Mary Evans Picture Library; Christies Images.

ISBN 0 75250 051 1

A copy of the British Library Cataloguing in Publication
Data is available from the British Library.

Typeset by Hewer Text Composition Services, Edinburgh
Printed in Singapore by Tien Wah Press

Contents

❧ LOVE ❧

I started early, took my dog,
  And visited the sea;
The mermaids in the basement
Came out to look at me,

And frigates in the upper floor
Extended hempen hands,
Presuming me to be a mouse
Aground, upon the sands.

But no man moved me till the tide
Went past my simple shoe,
And past my apron and my belt,
And past my bodice too,

And made as he would eat me up
As wholly as a dew
Upon a dandelion's sleeve –
And then I started too.

And he – he followed close behind;
I felt his silver heel
Upon my ankle, – then my shoes
Would overflow with pearl.

Until we met the solid town,
No man he seemed to know;
And bowing with a mighty look
At me, the sea withdrew.

I gave myself to him,
And took himself for pay.
The solemn contract of a life
Was ratified this way.

The wealth might disappoint,
Myself a poorer prove
Than this great purchaser suspect,
The daily own of Love

Depreciate the vision;
But, till the merchant buy,
Still fable, in the isles of spice,
The subtle cargoes lie.

At least, 'tis mutual risk, –
Some found it mutual gain;
Sweet debt of Life, – each night to owe,
Insolvent, every noon.

I see thee better in the dark,
I do not need a light.
The love of thee a prism be
Excelling, violet.

I see thee better for the years
That hunch themselves between,
The miner's lamp sufficient be
To nullify the mine.

And in the grave I see thee best —
Its little panels be
A-glow, all ruddy with the light
I held so high for thee!

What need of day to those whose dark
Hath so surpassing sun,
It deem it be continually
At the meridian?

I f you were coming in the fall,
I'd brush the summer by
With half a smile and half a spurn,
As housewives do a fly.

If I could see you in a year,
I'd wind the months in balls,
And put them each in separate drawers,
Until their time befalls.

If only centuries delayed,
I'd count them on my hand,
Subtracting till my fingers dropped
Into Van Diemen's land.

If certain, when this life was out,
That yours and mine should be,
I'd toss it yonder like a rind,
And taste eternity.

But now, all ignorant of the length
Of time's uncertain wing,
It goads me, like the goblin bee,
That will not state its sting.

T he love a life can show below,
Is but a filament, I know,
Of that diviner thing
That faints upon the face of noon
And smites the tinder in the sun
And hinders Gabriel's wing.

'Tis this in music hints and sways,
And far abroad on Summer days
Distills uncertain pain.
'Tis this enamors in the East.
And tints the transit in the West
With harrowing iodine.

'Tis this invites, appals, endows,
Flits, glimmers, proves, dissolves,
Returns, suggests, convicts, enchants –
Then flings in Paradise!

He touched me, so I live to know
    That such a day, permitted so,
I groped upon his breast.
It was a boundless place to me,
And silenced, as the awful sea
    Puts minor streams to rest.

And now, I'm different from before,
As if I breathed superior air,
    Or brushed a royal gown;
My feet, too, that had wandered so,
My gypsy face transfigured now
    To tenderer renown.

'Till death' is narrow loving;
The scantiest heart extant
Will hold you, till your privilege
Of finiteness be spent.

But he whose loss procures you
Such destitution that
Your life, too abject for itself,
Thenceforward imitate –

Until, resemblance perfect,
Yourself for his pursuit
Delight of nature abdicate,
Exhibit love somewhat.

I had not minded walls
Were Universe one rock,
And far I heard his silver call
The other side the block.

I'd tunnel until my groove
Pushed sudden through to his,
Then my face take recompense —
The looking in his eyes.

But 'tis a single hair,
A filament, a law —
A cobweb wove in adamant,
A battlement of straw —

A limit like the veil
Unto the lady's face,
But every mesh a citadel
And dragons in the crease!

To pile like Thunder to its close,
    Then crumble grand away,
While everything created hid –
This would be Poetry:
Or Love, – the two coeval came –
We both and neither prove,
Experience either, and consume –
For none see God and live.

That Love is all there is,
Is all we know of Love;
It is enough, the freight should be
Proportioned to the groove.

We outgrow love like other things
    And put it in the drawer,
Till it an antique fashion shows
    Like costumes grandsires wore.

★

We shall find the cube of the rainbow,
Of that there is no doubt;
But the arc of a lover's conjecture
Eludes the finding out.

I started early, took my dog,
And visited the sea

T he rose did caper on her cheek,
  Her bodice rose and fell,
Her pretty speech, like drunken men,
Did stagger pitiful.

Her fingers fumbled at her work, –
Her needle would not go;
What ailed so smart a little maid
It puzzled me to know,

Till opposite I spied a cheek
That bore another rose;
Just opposite, another speech
That like the drunkard goes;

A vest that, like the bodice, danced
To the immortal tune, –
Till those two troubled little clocks
Ticked softly into one.

❧ DEATH ❧

B ecause I could not stop for Death,
  He kindly stopped for me;
The carriage held but just ourselves
And Immortality.

We slowly drove, he knew no haste,
And I had put away
My labor, and my leisure too,
For his civility.

We passed the school where children played
At wrestling in a ring;
We passed the fields of gazing grain,
We passed the setting sun.

We paused before a house that seemed
A swelling of the ground;
The roof was scarcely visible,
The cornice but a mound.

Since then 'tis centuries; but each
Feels shorter than the day
I first surmised the horses' heads
Were toward eternity.

The distance that the dead have gone
    Does not at first appear;
Their coming back seems possible
    For many an ardent year.

And then, that we have followed them
    We more than half suspect,
So intimate have we become
    With their dear retrospect.

And now, I'm different from before,
As if I breathed superior air

The last night that she lived,
It was a common night,
Except the dying; this to us
Made nature different.

We noticed smallest things, —
Things overlooked before,
By this great light upon our minds
Italicized, as 'twere.

That others could exist
While she must finish quite,
A jealousy for her arose
So nearly infinite.

We waited while she passed;
It was a narrow time,
Too jostled were our souls to speak,
At length the notice came.

She mentioned, and forgot;
Then lightly as a reed
Bent to the water, shivered scarce,
Consented, and was dead.

And we, we placed the hair,
And drew the head erect;
And then an awful leisure was,
Our faith to regulate.

Her fingers fumbled at her work,
Her needle would not go

I died for beauty, but was scarce
Adjusted in the tomb,
When one who died for truth was lain
In an adjoining room.

He questioned softly why I failed?
'For beauty,' I replied.
'And I for truth, – the two are one;
We brethren are,' he said.

And so, as kinsmen met a night,
We talked between the rooms,
Until the moss had reached our lips,
And covered up our names.

I heard a fly buzz when I died;
    The stillness round my form
Was like the stillness in the air
    Between the heaves of storm.

The eyes beside had wrung them dry,
    And breaths were gathering sure
For that last onset, when the king
    Be witnessed in his power.

I willed my keepsakes, signed away
    What portion of me I
Could make assignable, – and then
    There interposed a fly,

With blue, uncertain, stumbling buzz,
    Between the light and me;
And then the windows failed, and then
    I could not see to see.

On this long storm the rainbow rose,
On this late morn the sun;
The clouds, like listless elephants,
Horizons straggled down.

The birds rose smiling in their nests,
The gales indeed were done;
Alas! how heedless were the eyes
On whom the summer shone!

The quiet nonchalance of death
No daybreak can bestir;
The slow archangel's syllables
Must awaken her.

This quiet Dust was Gentlemen and
    Ladies,
    And Lads and Girls;
Was laughter and ability and sighing,
    And frocks and curls.
This passive place a Summer's nimble mansion,
    Where Bloom and Bees
Fulfilled their Oriental Circuit,
    Then ceased like these.

The distance that the dead have gone
Does not at first appear

'T was just this time last year I died.
   I know I heard the corn,
When I was carried by the farms, —
   It had the tassels on.

I thought how yellow it would look
   When Richard went to mill;
And then I wanted to get out,
   But something held my will.

I thought just how red apples wedged
   The stubble's joints between;
And carts went stooping round the fields
   To take the pumpkins in.

I wondered which would miss me least,
    And when Thanksgiving came,
If father'd multiply the plates
    To make an even sum.

And if my stocking hung too high,
    Would it blur the Christmas glee,
That not a Santa Claus could reach
    The altitude of me?

But this sort grieved myself, and so
    I thought how it would be
When just this time, some perfect year,
Themselves should come to me.

The quiet nonchalance of death
No daybreak can bestir

❧ NATURE ❧

There's a certain slant of light,
   On winter afternoons,
That oppresses, like the weight
Of cathedral tunes.

Heavenly hurt it gives us;
We can find no scar,
But internal difference
Where the meanings are.

None may teach it anything,
'Tis the seal, despair, –
An imperial affliction
Sent us of the air.

When it comes, the landscape listens,
Shadows hold their breath;
When it goes, 'tis like the distance
On the look of death.

A something in a summer's day,
As slow her flambeaux burn away,
Which solemnizes me.

A something in a summer's noon, –
An azure depth, a wordless tune,
Transcending ecstasy.

And still within a summer's night
A something so transporting bright,
I clap my hands to see;

Then veil my too inspecting face,
Lest such a subtle, shimmering grace
Flutter too far for me.

The wizard–fingers never rest,
The purple brook within the breast
Still chafes its narrow bed;

Still rears the East her amber flag,
Guides still the sun along the crag
His caravan of red,

Like flowers that heard the tale of dews,
But never deemed the dripping prize
Awaited their low brows;

Or bees, that thought the summer's name
Some rumor of delirium
No summer could for them;

Or Arctic creature, dimly stirred
By tropic hint, – some travelled bird
Imported to the wood;

Or wind's bright signal to the ear,
Making that homely and severe,
Contented, known, before

The heaven unexpected came,
To lives that thought their worshipping
A too presumptuous psalm.

Young Boy by a Waterfall, John Singer Sargent

T he wind begun to rock the grass
   With threatening tunes and low, –
He flung a menace at the earth,
A menace at the sky.

The leaves unhooked themselves from trees
And started all abroad;
The dust did scoop itself like hands
And throw away the road.

The wagons quickened on the streets,
The thunder hurried slow;
The lightning showed a yellow beak,
And then a livid claw.

The birds put up the bars to nests,
The cattle fled to barns;
There came one drop of giant rain,
And then, as if the hands

That held the dams had parted hold,
The waters wrecked the sky,
But overlooked my father's house,
Just quartering a tree.

A vastness, as a neighbour, came,–
A wisdom without face or name

I dreaded that first robin so,
But he is mastered now,
And I'm accustomed to him grown, –
He hurts a little, though.

I thought if I could only live
Till that first shout got by,
Not all pianos in the woods
Had power to mangle me.

I dared not meet the daffodils,
For fear their yellow gown
Would pierce me with a fashion
So foreign to my own.

I wished the grass would hurry,
So when 'twas time to see,
He'd be too tall, the tallest one
Could stretch to look at me.

I could not bear the bees should come,
I wished they'd stay away
In those dim countries where they go:
What word had they for me?

They're here, though; not a creature failed,
No blossom stayed away
In gentle deference to me,
The Queen of Calvary.

Each one salutes me as he goes,
And I my childish plumes
Lift, in bereaved acknowledgment
Of their unthinking drums.

T he cricket sang,
　　And set the sun,
And workmen finished, one by one,
　　Their seam the day upon.

The low grass loaded with the dew,
The twilight stood as strangers do
With hat in hand, polite and new,
　　To stay as if, or go.

A vastness, as a neighbor, came, –
A wisdom without face or name,
A peace, as hemispheres at home, –
　　And so the night became.

The spider as an artist
    Has never been employed
Though his surpassing merit
  Is freely certified

By every broom and Bridget
    Throughout a Christian land.
Neglected son of genius,
   I take thee by the hand.

They're here, though: not a creature failed,
No blossom stayed away

We like March, his shoes are purple,
  He is new and high;
Makes he mud for dog and peddler,
  Makes he forest dry;
Knows the adder's tongue his coming,
  And begets her spot.
Stands the sun so close and mighty
  That our minds are hot.
News is he of all the others;
  Bold it were to die
With the blue-birds buccaneering
  On his British sky.

The clouds their backs together laid,
The north begun to push,
The forests galloped till they fell,
The lightning skipped like mice;
The thunder crumbled like a stuff –
How good to be safe in tombs,
Where nature's temper cannot reach,
Nor vengeance ever comes!

Exultation is the going
Of an inland soul to sea

The bat is dun with wrinkled wings
  Like fallow article,
And not a song pervades his lips,
  Or none perceptible.

His small umbrella, quaintly halved,
  Describing in the air
An arc alike inscrutable, –
  Elate philosopher!

Deputed from what firmament
  Of what astute abode,
Empowered with what malevolence
  Auspiciously withheld.

To his adroit Creator
  Ascribe no less the praise;
Beneficent, believe me,
  His eccentricities.

A sloop of amber slips away
    Upon an ether sea,
And wrecks in peace a purple tar,
    The son of ecstasy.

❧ THE SOUL ❧

A t leisure is the Soul
That gets a staggering blow;
The width of Life before it spreads
Without a thing to do.

It begs you give it work,
But just the placing pins –
Or humblest patchwork children do,
To help its vacant hands.

A dventure most unto itself
The Soul condemned to be;
Attended by a Single Hound –
Its own Identity.

The soul selects her own society,
Then shuts the door

The soul's distinct connection
With immortality
Is best disclosed by danger,
Or quick calamity, –

As lightning on a landscape
Exhibits sheets of place
Not yet suspected but for flash
And bolt and suddenness.

The Soul's superior instants
Occur to Her alone,
When friend and earth's occasion
Have infinite withdrawn.

Or she, Herself, ascended
To too remote a height,
For lower recognition
Than Her Omnipotent.

Under the Moon Beams, Atkinson Grimshaw

This mortal abolition
Is seldom, but as fair
As Apparition – subject
To autocratic air.

Eternity's disclosure
To favorites, a few,
Of the Colossal substance
Of immortality.

I felt a funeral in my brain,
   And mourners, to and fro,
Kept treading, treading, till it seemed
   That sense was breaking through.

And when they all were seated,
   A service like a drum
Kept beating, beating, till I thought
   My mind was going numb.

And then I heard them lift a box,
  And creak across my soul
With those same boots of lead, again.
  Then space began to toll

As all the heavens were a bell,
  And Being but an ear,
And I and silence some strange race,
  Wrecked, solitary, here.

He fumbles at your spirit
  As players at the keys
Before they drop full music on;
  He stuns you by degrees,

Prepares your brittle substance
  For the ethereal blow,
By fainter hammers, further heard,
  Then nearer, then so slow

Your breath has time to straighten,
  Your brain to bubble cool, –
Deals one imperial thunderbolt
  That scalps your naked soul.

Summer Flowers, William John Wainwright

E xultation is the going
Of an inland soul to sea, –
Past the houses, past the headlands,
Into deep eternity!

Bred as we, among the mountains,
Can the sailor understand
The divine intoxication
Of the first league out from land?

The soul selects her own society,
  Then shuts the door;
On her divine majority
Obtrude no more.

Unmoved, she notes the chariot's pausing
At her low gate;
Unmoved, an emperor is kneeling
Upon her mat.

I've known her from an ample nation
Choose one;
Then close the valves of her attention
Like stone.

The Maid with the Golden Hair, Frederick,
Lord Leighton

The soul unto itself
Is an imperial friend, —
Or the most agonizing spy
An enemy could send.

Secure against its own.
No treason it can fear:
Itself its sovereign, of itself
The soul should stand in awe.

&ospraey; LIFE &ospraey;

M uch madness is divinest sense
  To a discerning eye;
Much sense the starkest madness.

'Tis the majority
In this, as all, prevails.
Assent, and you are sane;
Demur, – you're straightway dangerous,
And handled with a chain.

M y life closed twice before its close;
    It yet remains to see
If Immortality unveil
    A third event to me,

So huge, so hopeless to conceive,
    As these that twice befell.
Parting is all we know of heaven,
    And all we need of hell.

I years had been from home,
And now, before the door,
I dared not open, lest a face
I never saw before

Stare vacant into mine
And ask my business there.
My business, – just a life I left,
Was such still dwelling there?

I fumbled at my nerve,
I scanned the windows near;
The silence like an ocean rolled,
And broke against my ear.

For each ecstatic instant
We must an anguish pay

I laughed a wooden laugh
That I could fear a door,
Who danger and the dead had faced,
But never quaked before.

I fitted to the latch
My hand, with trembling care,
Lest back the awful door should spring,
And leave me standing there.

I moved my fingers off
As cautiously as glass,
And held my ears, and like a thief
Fled gasping from the house.

It was not death, for I stood up,
And all the dead lie down;
It was not night, for all the bells
Put out their tongues, for noon.

It was not frost, for on my flesh
I felt siroccos crawl, –
Nor fire, for just my marble feet
Could keep a chancel cool.

And yet it tasted like them all;
The figures I have seen
Set orderly, for burial,
Reminded me of mine,

Wandering Thoughts, William Powell Frith

As if my life were shaven
And fitted to a frame,
And could not breathe without a key;
And 'twas like midnight, some,

When everything that ticked has stopped,
And space stares, all around,
Or grisly frosts, first autumn morns,
Repeal the beating ground.

But most like chaos, – stopless, cool, –
Without a chance or spar,
Or even a report of land
To justify despair.

They say that 'time assuages,'
    Time never did assuage:
An actual suffering strengthens,
    As sinews do, with age.

Time is a test of trouble,
    But not a remedy.
If such it prove, it prove too
    There was no malady.

F aith is a fine invention
  For gentlemen who see;
But microscopes are prudent
In an emergency!

F or each ecstatic instant
We must an anguish pay
In keen and quivering ratio
To the ecstasy.

For each beloved hour
Sharp pittances of years,
Bitter contested farthings
And coffers heaped with tears.

When everything that ticked has stopped,
And space stares, all around

S uccess is counted sweetest
By those who ne'er succeed.
To comprehend a nectar
Requires sorest need.

Not one of all the purple host
Who took the flag to-day
Can tell the definition,
So clear, of victory,

As he, defeated, dying,
On whose forbidden ear
The distant strains of triumph
Break, agonized and clear.

A fter great pain a formal feeling comes –
　　The nerves sit ceremonious like tombs;
The stiff Heart questions – was it He that bore?
And yesterday – or centuries before?

The feet mechanical
Go round a wooden way
Of ground or air Ought, regardless grown,
A quartz contentment like a stone.

This is the hour of lead
Remembered if outlived,
As freezing persons recollect the snow –
First chill, then stupor, then the letting go.

I took one draught of life,
  I'll tell you what I paid,
Precisely an existence –
The market price, they said.

They weighed me, dust by dust,
They balanced film with film,
Then handed me my being's worth –
A single dram of Heaven.

A word is dead
When it is said,
  Some say.
I say it just
Begins to live
  That day.

❧ ETERNITY ❧

This world is not conclusion;
 A sequel stands beyond,
Invisible, as music,
 But positive, as sound.
It beckons and it baffles;
 Philosophies don't know,

And through a riddle, at the last,
 Sagacity must go.
To guess it puzzles scholars;
 To gain it, men have shown
Contempt of generations.
 And crucifixion known.

I s Heaven a physician?
   They say that He can heal;
But medicine posthumous
   Is unavailable.

Is Heaven an exchequer?
   They speak of what we owe;
But that negociation
   I'm not a party to.

I mmortal is an ample word
    When what we need is by,
But when it leaves us for a time,
    'Tis a necessity.

Of heaven above the firmest proof
    We fundamental know,
Except for its marauding hand,
    It had been heaven below.

I never saw a moor,
I never saw the sea;
Yet know I how the heather looks,
And what a wave must be.

I never spoke with God,
Nor visited in heaven;
Yet certain am I of the spot
As if the chart were given.

Our journey had advanced;
  Our feet were almost come
To that odd fork in Being's road,
Eternity by term.

Our pace took sudden awe,
Our feet reluctant led.
Before were cities, but between,
The forest of the dead.

Retreat was out of hope, –
Behind, a sealéd route,
Eternity's white flag before,
And God at every gate.

H eaven is what I cannot reach!
    The apple on the tree,
Provided it do hopless hang,
    That 'heaven' is, to me.

The color on the cruising cloud,
    The interdicted ground
Behind the hill, the house behind, –
    There Paradise is found!

I shall know why, when time is over,
And I have ceased to wonder why;
Christ will explain each separate anguish
In the fair schoolroom of the sky.

He will tell me what Peter promised,
And I, for wonder at his woe,
I shall forget the drop of anguish
That scalds me now, that scalds me now.

J ust lost when I was saved!
  Just felt the world go by!
Just girt me for the onset with eternity,
When breath blew back,
And on the other side
I heard recede the disappointed tide!

Therefore, as one returned, I feel,
Odd secrets of the line to tell!
Some sailor, skirting foreign shores,
Some pale reporter from the awful doors
Before the seal!

Next time, to stay!
Next time, the things to see
By ear unheard,
Unscrutinized by eye.

Next time, to tarry,
While the ages steal, –
Slow tramp the centuries,
And the cycles wheel.